No One Wronged Me... More Than Me

A young girl's guide to stopping the cycle of self-neglect, and to embrace self-love.

Pamela Renee Gunn

No One Has Wronged me…More Than Me
ISBN: DIGITAL VERSION

All scriptures use the King James Version unless otherwise notated within the text.

Paraphrased quote derived from: Neuroscience Explains Why Instagram Is So Bad for Teen Girls, by Nicole Fisher, founder and President of Health and Human Rights Strategies, Forbes Magazine, June 30, 2019

All other quotes and references were derived from a public domain and have been cited within the text.

Dedication

Transparency is not always easy. I pray this offering helps to free young girls who may struggle with a lack of self-worth, low self-esteem, or a lack of self-love. My prayer is that young girls may know, accept, and embrace their inner strength (even in their youth), so that they may experience the freedom of self-expression and self-love, for it is the best gift to give.

I pray my story helps to reveal God's glory! If he did it for me, he can do it again for you! My prayers are for you to be blessed through my journey, by my story and through my testimony.

A letter to my children

To my children, every day I strive to keep my cup full so that I can pour into your life and teach you the importance of self-love and self-belief. My prayers are for you to know who you are and to celebrate your uniqueness, your beauty, and your inner strength. I pray that God allows you to become fully emerged in your purpose even at a young age, so that He can use you to **change the world.**

Words from the Author

As a little girl, I struggled with low self-esteem. I didn't love myself; I didn't know what it was or how to do so. I thought I was ugly because I was a brown skinned girl.

When it came to thought patterns about myself, I absolutely carried the worst. I know what you are thinking, how can you learn those behaviors as a child? Well, for starters, self-love wasn't a topic of discussion in my household. Perhaps, self-hate was a behavior passed down. I carried self-loathing thoughts about myself. Thoughts such as, "I always get treated wrong" or "I always get the bad end of the stick". Those thoughts were my expectations and the energy I attracted to myself. Those thoughts became my reality. My thoughts were so dark, they became suicidal.

Those thoughts carried into my adulthood and into my life experiences-at home, at work, in relationships, etc. I naturally placed myself last in almost all situations. I would justify this behavior as humility! What I didn't realize was that I was cheating myself. I was cheating myself because I didn't love myself. What I didn't realize was that I needed to love others, the way that I loved myself, and my self-reflection, directly correlated to the way others saw me.

I started my journey of self-love and self-acceptance around the time I started college and met my boyfriend who is now my husband. It was during this time, that I went through a process of healing and a coming into my femininity and womanhood. I had to do some serious self-reflections and self-evaluations.

My spiritual foundation is and has always been Christianity. So, as I was reading my bible I ran across this verse, *Love your neighbors as yourself* in Mark 12:31. It literally changed my life; the second greatest commandment! The words were simply illuminating, and I had an understanding like never before!

When you love yourself, you are keeping your cup full! You are able to express love in its highest form. I thought, how could I be happy for others, when I am not happy for myself? How can I be genuine to others, when I am not genuine with myself? How can I love others, when I don't love myself? To want for others what you want for self has to be followed with a prerequisite of self-love.

I started to declare those words over my life. I began to pay attention to my thoughts, and I decided to change my thought patterns and to change the language that I was speaking about myself. I was extremely careful about the words I used about myself and wouldn't allow others to speak less than. Words are powerful!

Thoughts are too, because they become your words! I treated myself without feeling guilty! I dated myself, and healed myself from my past, by accepting the good and bad in my life! I spent time alone with myself! Solace and peace were necessary for me. I started appreciating the beauty deep within! I went through an emotional process of self-forgiveness. I had to heal the little girl on the inside in order to fully embrace my womanhood.

Moreover, I spoke to myself daily and prayed a prayer of forgiveness over my life. Once I embraced this powerful lesson, my atmosphere changed! My confidence grew, and the people around me changed. Things started to get better and better. As I reflect, I believe in my heart that it was destined for me to come into my truth before I gave birth to my children! God allowed me to first heal before I conceived my daughters and son!

Healing takes place, prior to conception

Our ability to love is often based on the way we love ourselves! I am really big on the law of attraction. Let us be mindful of how we love and treat ourselves as it pertains to our connections and relationships! Speak words of positivity into the universe and watch the positive impact it makes!

Queens, when we embrace who we are and stop cheating ourselves (When you allow others to cheat you, you are really cheating yourself), we begin to embrace the most powerful thing God gave us. Our femininity and womanhood! Our femininity is not about pink roses and flowers; it is about embracing who we are as WOMEN! It's about loving who we are and every fiber of our being. There is a saying that says, "Heal the man, you heal the land"! This is true! And this also reigns true in my heart... "The rise of the Woman is the rise of the nation". We are nurturers and we are the vehicles through which birthing takes place. That's powerful! When you embrace your power, you loose the chains of brokenness. Love yourselves first, so that you can give love freely!

Introduction

In the age of smartphones, social media, followers, and likes, validation in our young people is increasingly associated with online approval. Our young girls are exposed to many things on a greater level than my generation. Instagram will have you comparing yourself with others in an unhealthy way, if you aren't careful. This unhealthy comparison leads to damaging thoughts regarding how we feel about ourselves.

Society's standard of beauty shapes the way we feel about ourselves. This in turn, contributes to more anxiety and depression due to feelings of inadequacy, low self-esteem and feelings of unworthiness.

According to an article in Forbes magazine written by Nicole Fisher, founder and President of Health and Human Rights Strategies, she writes about the impact of social media on young people. In the article, she explains that our girls are growing up with unrealistic ideas of what beauty is. This is largely due to increased exposure to "idealized" images of other women, couples, and lives in general. Increased exposure is linked to decreased happiness with one's own life. For example, filters, makeup, lighting, angles and posing mean that the images consistently fed to young girls are not based in reality. Instagram posts blur reality. With the increased number of young girls having goals to becoming Instagram models, the imagery of what is real becomes distorted. Our young people are up against some unrealistic expectations.

That is why I wrote this book, to share my story. My concern is that our young people especially young girls are not getting the tools or proper teaching of self-love and self-worth. As a result, many of our youth may struggle with self-identity and self-love because of what is considered acceptable in society. Our young people are exposed to a false sense of reality in terms of beauty standards and are struggling with their own identity.

As a young girl, I was very critical of myself. Self-sabotage became a way that I talked myself out of doing a lot of things that I loved. Simply put, I didn't know the value of my self-esteem nor did I have confidence. That is why I wrote this book with hopes that this offering will help to free young people from the heavy weight of unworthiness and not knowing who they are. Belief in yourself will allow your gifts to flourish into a world where it's desperately needed!

My healing began with an honest conversation and assessment of myself. A conversation I had with myself and with God. I started to dig deeper by asking God to show me, ME. I wanted to understand why things were happening the way they were. I wanted to change the way I was being treated by others and I wanted to change the way I was treating myself. I kept noticing a pattern. I asked God to reveal to me how to attract the type of love I desired. God spoke and it was a healing revelation. The understanding was that, how I treated myself was a direct reflection of how others treated me. I wanted to understand this more about how I treated myself, instead of how others treated me. It took a great deal of courage and intentionality, but knowledge of self was the best revelation I received. I will share with you those healing revelations.

As the title says, No One Has Wronged Me, More Than Me, I had to realize that I was the key to unlocking my own happiness. It was ME versus ME all along. No one could treat me at a higher level than I was treating myself. Healing began to take place with this realization. When I realized that in order to stop the cycle, healing began with me!

By not expecting anyone else to treat me any less than I would treat myself, I began to show myself the love that I desired. I realized that if I didn't value myself, how could I expect others to value me. If I didn't have self-respect, how could I expect others to respect me?

As the saying goes, you attract the energy that you give off. You are responsible for letting others know how you want to be treated. We sometimes allow other people to treat us like we are not worthy of love, simply because we haven't learned what it means to truly love ourselves.

In the forthcoming chapters, I take you on a journey of how I allowed self-sabotage to control the way I thought about myself. I am sharing my story with hopes that it will compel you to think about how you treat yourself so that you will fully embrace your highest self. I am sharing my story of how a lack of self-love allowed me to have an abusive relationship with myself. Fear and lack of self-confidence had me bound. I share my story with hopes that this offering; my testimony, will help you, while yet in your youth, to know and believe, and to hold on to this very belief system, YOU ARE WORTHY! YOU ARE ENOUGH! Get ready to make your mark in this world.

Affirmation

I love myself deeply and completely

I accept my strengths and my weaknesses

I show love to myself daily

I forgive myself for not seeing my own worth

I am confident

I am loved

I am healed

Music is My Solace

Music is and has always been healing and therapeutic for me. Music played a powerful role in my life as a little girl. I was in love with music. Music was my solace. Music was my peace. I started writing music and creating tunes in my head at an early age. Even before I knew I could sing, I loved to sing.

My love affair with music, as I can remember, started around five years of age. My most vivid memory was of me sitting on the porch in the projects, writing songs to the theme music of the ice cream truck that rode down my street. I wrote about love and boys and all of the important stuff that little girls at my age would sing about. I loved to write songs. Music was my friend; it kept me smiling, made me hopeful, and whenever music was present, I was in a good space.

One of my early musical influences was the Queen of Pop, Whitney Houston. I sat on my steps and enjoyed being in my happy place; with music. I imagined being on stage performing songs, encouraging others, and making others feel what I felt. Listening to Whitney gave me an escape from the harsh reality of growing up in poverty and living in the projects.

My love for music was strong and I knew I had a talent for singing; however, I hadn't activated my gift. I was extremely shy about singing and very particular about it. So, I shared my gift with no one. All I knew was, whenever I felt it, I would express it. Unless you lived in the same household, you probably wouldn't have ever known that I had a love for singing, or that I loved music.

As a little girl, I sang in the Children's choir at Fourth Street Missionary Baptist Church. This is where I learned to harmonize, and I enjoyed learning new songs and singing praise and worship songs. I still had not developed the confidence to embrace my gifts and talent, yet creativity and my imagination were my ways of expressing myself.

I was a vivid daydreamer, and music afforded me short-term escape from my reality. I always knew that I was a deep thinker and very intuitive. I was labeled the sensitive one. To be able to feel so very deeply, at that time, was something I didn't understand. I thought it was a weakness. I thought my sensitivity was me being weak, but I later learned that being able to feel deeply and express myself, was a sought-after strength. I wouldn't come to fully understand this as a blessing until womanhood. *I didn't know my own strength.*

My dad was a huge influence. He sang this one song in particular to me and my sisters. We would sing it all of the time; *"Holy Spirit, we welcome you, in this place tonight, come and set my spirit free and make everything all right, feel me with your loving joy and strengthen me by your might, Holy Spirit, we welcome you, in this place tonight."* I never actually knew the title of this song or who wrote it and for a long time, I thought it was written and produced by my daddy. We would sing this song with daddy as if this was the only song on the face of this earth. I got embarrassed when he made us sing it in front of people. Oh, how I wish I could sing that song with Daddy just one more time.

Daddy was our backbone; he was truly one of a kind. Growing up, I was very shy about sharing my talent. My daddy was instrumental in breaking me out of my shyness. Because I was very shy as a little girl, I was often too scared to sing in front of others. The older I got, the more I hid my talent, I didn't share it, and I kept it to myself. I buried it in a sacred place. Although I loved music, I didn't believe in myself nor did I embrace my talent enough to believe that I could do anything with it. I wasn't taught to embrace it, to love it, to nurture it, and to share it. I didn't know how to. I thought if I couldn't sing like the next person, then I wasn't good enough.

This was the beginning of what would become my way of self-sabotage, and not believing in myself. Because I compared myself with others, I neglected my own talent. This attitude and way of thinking followed me throughout my childhood and crippled me from seeing my worth. I didn't think I was talented enough or worthy of this gift. Perhaps, I wasn't told enough, that I was enough. This attitude was only the beginning of more damaging thoughts I had of myself. I didn't know my worth!

Let's Look Within!

How can we as mentors, teachers, role models, and parents, teach our girls to embrace who they are?

_____

_____

_____

_____

_____

_____

_____

_____

_____

In what ways have you experienced self-neglect?

_____

_____

_____

_____

_____

_____

_____

_____

_____

What do you like about you?

_____

_____

_____

_____

_____

_____

_____

_____

_____

_____

What are some negative beliefs about yourself that
you have created?

_____

_____

_____

_____

_____

_____

_____

Dear Divine,

I love you with all of my Heart, Mind, and Soul.

Thank you for the gifts and talents that you have given to me.

May I use them to bring you glory!

Give me the courage to let my light shine.

You accept me where there is self-neglect!

Put a new song on my heart! Fill me with the lyrics of your love!

Amen!

Affirmations

I am worthy of love,

success and happiness

I walk in confidence

knowing that everything I need

to make my dreams come true is in my hands

Self-Esteem

"How can I, Love somebody else, if I can't love myself enough to know when it's time, time to let go"

-Mary J. Blige

Have you ever received a gift that you didn't care for, so you put it someplace you know you'd forget? Well, I was gifted with a gift and talent that I did not appreciate. I did not nurture it and I didn't think I was valuable enough to receive it. Because of the way I felt about myself, I didn't think I was worthy enough of this gift. I had big dreams and a deep desire to sing. But I didn't love my voice. And because of this lack of love for self, I didn't cultivate it as I should have, so I placed singing on the back burner. I hadn't learned to love my authentic voice. In fact, I was my own biggest critic. I didn't like the way I sounded. Why? Because I was operating on some very low self-esteem. My sense of self was challenged during my early years. It led me to comparing myself with others.

Comparison is the thief of joy

23

Comparison is a dream killer, and unhealthy self-esteem will have you comparing yourself (unnecessarily) with others. I would know. Growing up in a household with siblings, it's quite natural to compare yourself to your siblings. Competition among siblings can teach you about healthy competition in real life. In fact, sibling rivalry is real, whether blatant or subtle. And if this rivalry is not guarded and used in a positive way, it could definitely lead to an unhealthy relationship with self.

Growing up with five siblings (Three younger sisters, and two older brothers), you learn to hold your own. We all competed for mama's attention. We were all spaced in age, so our sibling rivalry was more subtle. We all had different personalities and talents. However, we were never taught how to honor each other's differences and talents.

Because my self-esteem was compromised, I was more reluctant to share my talent at an early age. I compared myself to my sister, who was more outgoing. And even though, I loved to sing, it made me draw back from singing. I was developing my own sense of worth based on how I stacked up against my sister. This comparison was so unhealthy. It made me withdraw when it came to sharing my talent and I felt in some way, there wasn't room for me. My self-esteem was something I did not consider or attempt to improve back then.

Healthy self-esteem creates the pathway to walking in your purpose and gift activation. Self-esteem is your evaluation of your own worth, it is what you believe about yourself, what you think about yourself and how you see yourself. Healthy esteem is seeing ourselves in a positive way. How YOU see yourself is key. The evaluation of oneself, starts with a voice. The words that we hear about ourselves shapes how we see ourselves. The words that we speak about ourselves gives birth to our self-identity. Positive affirmations are important! We have power to speak life or to speak death. Provers 18:21, reads, *life and death are in the power of our tongues.*

My self-esteem began to rise when I changed the very words that I spoke of myself and I was starting to learn how to use my own voice. Your voice matters. The words we hear growing up, can become our inner voice over time. Words determine how we see ourselves; it shapes our self-esteem. That's why it is so important to filter the voices, whether they give us life or are used to break us down.

Too often we listen to the voice of others to shape who we are. If we are not careful to raise our self-esteem, we will make decisions that we are not proud of. Healthy self-esteem influences the choices and decisions we make. Before making a decision, ensure you are in a good place with yourself. Do a self-check and ask yourself, *am I honoring me with this decision?*

The decisions we make, gives way to the consequences of our choices. Your worthiness is rooted in healthy self-esteem. Your esteem can make or break you. It can serve as a tool to keep you stuck or to catapult you to expand into your full potential.

Because of this unhealthy relationship I had with myself as a young girl, self-sabotage became a way I would talk myself out of reaching any goals. Self-sabotage is when we actively take steps to talk ourselves out of walking in our fullest potential. I did this through self-doubt and negative self-talk. I lived the cliché, *too good to be true, because* I believed that if something was good, then it wasn't true, so I talked myself out of receiving what was good for me.

Several things can have a negative effect on your self-esteem. The experiences you had growing up, the relationships you had with your parents, and all can affect your self-esteem. It can have a ripple effect creating self-doubt, negative self-talk and feelings of unworthiness. That's why healing yourself by increasing yourself esteem is paramount.

Unhealthy self-esteem will have you seeking alternative ways to fill a void or to mask your pain. I was around 14 when I started smoking marijuana heavily. And as a teenager, I fell into that space of wanting to be high all the time. The reason behind me smoking was rooted in low self-esteem. I smoked to deal with my social anxiety. I felt that when I was around people,

I needed to be high in order to be myself. I relied on external factors to feel comfortable with myself. It gave me false confidence. I smoked during my high school years and even through college. In college, I would get high to ease the stress before taking exams in school. I stopped smoking for a while, to heal this part of me that relied on external factors to make me feel good about myself. Healing began as I looked within and started to dig deeper.

Raising myself esteem was a concerted effort, a conscious decision. I began to heal myself and increase my self-esteem through self-love. Self-love represented a child-like love in my eyes. I would visualize how I would love myself and it was as if I was my own child. I began to ask; *how would you treat yourself as a little child? How would you love yourself, nourish yourself, speak to yourself, and be real with yourself?*

Raising my self-esteem meant, unlearning some negative thought patterns and the belief systems I created. I had to learn that there is room for us all to shine! This was a big revelation for me to learn as a young girl. *Just like the stars in the sky, there is enough room in the universe for all of the stars to shine.* There is room. I had to unlearn this limiting belief system that says, if someone else is doing the same thing that you love, that means you can't do it! This belief system is simply untrue. I had to unlearn these behaviors through my self-love journey.

Let's Look Within!

When you look in the mirror, what do you see?

_____

_____

_____

_____

_____

_____

_____

_____

_____

How would you treat yourself as a little child? How would you love yourself, nourish yourself, speak to yourself, and be real with yourself?

_____

_____

_____

_____

_____

_____

_____

_____

_____

What would you like to change about yourself?

_____

_____

_____

_____

_____

_____

_____

_____

_____

What do you love about your family and friends?

_____

_____

_____

_____

_____

_____

_____

_____

_____

_____

What makes you happy?

_____

_____

_____

_____

_____

_____

_____

_____

_____

_____

_____

_____

_____

_____

_____

_____

_____

Dear Divine,

I love you with all of my heart, mind soul and strength.

Help me to see ME as you see ME

Help me to see the beauty and strength that lies within me.

Amen!

Self-Love Affirmations

Make the mirror your best friend and say these words often to yourself

I love me

I appreciate me

I value me

I support me

I like me

I am happy with me

I don't need other's validation

Self-Love

"Learning to Love Yourself is the Greatest Love of All"

-Whitney Houston

Loving yourself is a big deal. A pretty big deal. This affirmation was a complete game changer for me. It changed the way I felt about myself. I really hadn't grasp what it meant to truly love myself until adulthood. I remember praying and asking God to deliver me from the same situations that seemed to keep me in the same situations, time after time. I asked several questions, perhaps the most important question was, why does this keep happening to me? I was unhappy in my career, I was working towards my master's degree and it seemed I was on the perfect pathway to success, yet there was a fire inside that just wouldn't die.

I remember the Spirit spoke to me and I read Mark 12:31 about the second greatest command to *Love your neighbor as yourself*. It was as if a light bulb suddenly came on. You see, it was as if my life was a broken

33

record. It seemed I was stuck in a loop and my situation simply kept repeating itself. I kept repeating the same cycle, never learning the lesson. I was so ready to learn the lesson. I asked for wisdom and understanding. In other words, I was asking, what lesson do I need to learn?

The Prerequisite

Mark 12:31 The second is this; Love your neighbor as yourself' No other commandment is greater than these.

The command does not say to love other people more than you love yourself. Jesus taught that the second greatest command was to love our neighbors as we love ourselves. Meaning, we should love others just like we love ourselves. I love to be around people who have learned to value themselves, those who understand their worth and have knowledge of self. Their energy is different, the conversation is different. It takes a great deal of courage to look in the mirror and to examine our own selves, to consider the things that need changing. Those things that we identify needing change, are what we take to God in Prayer. *Show me, ME lord! In Jesus name I pray, amen.* This is a simple prayer, yet so profound.

Oftentimes we are so quick to point out other people's faults, that we are blind to our own shortcomings. My desire is to love others, as I love myself. I pray that as you continue in life's Journey, that you will gain the wisdom and understanding of self (know your value, your worth and know who it is that you belong to). I pray that you start loving yourself. Make this world a better place. When you love yourself, you are capable of letting your light shine, and embracing and nurturing your gifts and talents. Let your light shine, a city on a hill cannot be hidden!

Self-love is not all about treating yourself at the spa or how well you dress, and it goes beyond the aesthetic makeup. The term, self-love, has become a cliché, often used equivocally. Self-love is about your love of self, especially regarding your very own happiness. Self-love is a prerequisite for our ability to properly love others. It is the key to the universe. It is true, how we treat others is a reflection of what's going on with us internally.

How you treat yourself is a reflection of how others will ultimately treat you. When you are in the presence of others think about how they make you feel. Do you feel uplifted? Is there a positive vibe? Do you feel that this person brings you peace? Likewise, the vibe you get from others is also a direct reflection of how they, in turn love themselves.

Self-love is not selfish. Although there are times when we think of being conceited or vein, upon the thought of self-love, that just isn't the case. True self love is something we all need in order to become the best version of ourselves. The root of almost all of our personal problems stems from not loving ourselves. Self-love helps you to make better decisions. When I started my journey of self-love, I was open to receiving what God had for me. Through this journey, I was able to gain a better understanding of who I really was on the inside.

God revealed to me the harm that I was doing to myself through self-hate. Because I didn't understand why a lot of things were happening to me and around me, I started to ask questions. I was seeking growth and was tired of repeating the cycle. I was in a loop, I found myself going through the same old situations and the same circumstances and I finally asked God, how can I break this cycle? What lesson do I need to learn? I asked for wisdom to gain understanding

Not only did I place my talent and my gift on the back burner, I place myself on the back burner. I no longer had this fire and passion for music. I attempted to distract my mind through burying myself in other things such as school, I put all of my efforts into my studies neglecting my gifts and the need to love myself. Yet and still, this fire would not die within my soul. I still had this longing to walk in my calling and utilize my gift. I went on to college and continued to sing in jazz bands, in the choir, and I even obtained a music scholarship, however, I still dimmed my light.

How others saw me, was a reflection of how I viewed myself. How I treated myself impacted the way I allowed others to treat me. I carried this energy around with me even through adulthood and it followed me everywhere. I was consumed with feelings of unworthiness. On the job, I felt like I wasn't walking in my calling. I felt that I was always coming in second place.

I asked the question

One day I asked God a question, why do people treat me this way? I received the most powerful and liberating answer. I had an epiphany that it was my lack of self-love! If I started to love myself, I would see a change. I realized that self-love was the key and it was the answer to my question. This was my aha moment! Here was my revelation; the way I treated myself was teaching others how to treat me. God revealed to me that if I wanted change, I had to focus on ME. God knows how to bring it back to the root of the problem, which always start with you.

I am the energy that I attract. Once I began to look at the ways that I treated myself and all those years of self-sabotage that I placed on myself, I realized that I needed to make a change. I started treating myself better. I gave more attention to the very words that I spoke to myself. I realized that I put myself through so much. I held myself back so many times until I realized it was all because of this powerful word; LOVE, which is the highest vibration. I realize that because I didn't fully understand how to love myself, I didn't understand how to value myself, and I didn't see my worth.

We are living in an age now where understanding your self-identity is challenging, because there is so much shown on social media. Social media can be dangerous to some young girls because of the amount of information that they are exposed to. The things that they are exposed to makes it more challenging to accept themselves.

Self- love is about your own well-being and happiness. Doing what you need to do for your well-being, mentally, spiritually or physically. Many times, as young women we are conditioned to put others before ourselves. Women are natural nurturer and the most challenging part about that is, we sometimes forget ourselves. Pressures from social media creates a false sense of self-identity. Society teaches us to put others before we help ourselves. We place too much pressure on ourselves in order to make others happy. Society will have us putting pressure on ourselves at the expense of our own happiness.

Let's Look Within!

When was the last time you showed yourself some love and how?

_____

_____

_____

_____

_____

_____

_____

_____

_____

What words or beliefs do you live your life by?

_____

_____

_____

_____

_____

_____

_____

_____

_____

_____

_____

_____

_____

_____

What is the most loving thing you have ever done for yourself?

_____

_____

_____

_____

_____

_____

_____

_____

What is your biggest struggle with loving yourself?

_____

_____

_____

_____

_____

_____

_____

_____

_____

What do you need to do for YOU today?

_____

_____

_____

_____

_____

_____

_____

_____

_____

_____

_____

_____

_____

Self-Love Prayer

Dear Divine,

Let the <u>love</u> I have for myself be so strong that I never reject myself again.

Never sabotage my happiness, freedom, and <u>love</u>.

Let the power of my <u>self-love</u> be strong enough to cancel out all the lies that I tell myself such as; I am not strong enough,

good enough,

not worthy, and I cannot make it.

I am worthy of love!

Self-Acceptance Affirmations

By respecting **myself**,

I teach others to respect me.

By honoring **myself**,

I require that others honor me.

I believe I am worthy,

and my beliefs about **myself**

are more important to me

than the beliefs of others.

Self-Acceptance

"I am not my hair, I am not this skin, I am not your expectations no.... I am the soul that lives within."

-India Arie

India Arie; one of my favorite artists, inspired me to love who I am, exactly as I am. Her lyrics helped me to heal a part of myself that needed healing. The journey into womanhood was a beautiful journey and I was just beginning to understand what it meant to love myself. Although I was just beginning to put self-love into action, there was still a part of me that struggled with accepting the things I didn't like about myself. The song, *Not My Hair* was released when I was just graduating from College. The lyrics were birthed out of a woman losing her hair due to chemotherapy. The woman who inspired these lyrics accepted herself even after losing her hair from chemotherapy and still celebrated her beauty within. This is when I realize that what it meant to accept myself flaws and all. Self-acceptance is an attitude.

Heal me, Oh Lord, and I will be healed! –Jeremiah 17:14

Self-acceptance is all about embracing your strengths and weaknesses. It is when you are realistic about your evaluation of your talent, your capabilities and your worthiness. When you accept yourself, you adopt those feelings of satisfaction with your*self* despite your faults and deficiencies, regardless of past behaviors, choices and mistakes you've made.

When you accept yourself, you free yourself from the weight of guilt. You don't allow yourself to feel guilty from past mistakes, knowingly, those mistakes were necessary to teach and build your future self. Self-acceptance is the acceptance of all of your attributes, positive or negative. It includes body acceptance, self-protection from negative criticism, and believing in your capacities, talents, and gifts. Self-acceptance is a higher expression of love.

When I was younger, my self-esteem fluctuated. I thought highly of myself in some areas, and other areas, not so much. I was competent and confidence in some areas, and then still there were other things about myself where I was insecure. As life happens, we see changes in our self-esteem. Comparison contributes to the fluctuation of our esteem. Comparison says you don't accept who you are. When you compare yourself to others you are then telling yourself, "I don't accept who I am".

45

As an adult, I still struggle with insecurities and there are things about myself that I have to come to terms with accepting. For example, weight has always been a struggle for me. In the past, I also struggled with accepting other flaws and imperfections. I was self-conscious about my body, I had acne and when my face would break out, it made me so self-conscious. However today, I have the power and the tools to focus on the things I can change instead of focusing on flaws and imperfections. I thought that those things made me who I was until I learned the lesson- *it didn't.* When I struggled with low self-esteem, those insecurities made me feel unattractive and I carried a lot of insecurities because of that. When I learned to accept the person, God made me to be, I was then able to accept my beauty and see those things as a part of who I am. I was still beautiful despite my flaws. It did not change who I was on the inside. I am the soul that lives within.

God gives us exactly what we need to live out our dreams and to walk in our purpose. We grow up thinking we need to obtain "things" before we can pursue our dreams, but everything we need is on the inside of us. As a child, I was blessed with the gift of creativity. I loved all things art! I loved to dance, sing, and I loved everything about artistry. I loved fashion and I love to write songs and poems! I even designed dresses for my dolls and entered into talent shows, unafraid. I felt free as a bird because I had everything that I needed on the inside of me and was free from self-hate. I was free from the self-hate.

Once fear sets in, it entangles you and allows you to believe that you are not enough. Fear and doubt are dream killers. I started comparing myself with others and that comparison made me forget who I was. I became reluctant to do a lot of things because I didn't think I was good enough. I cared about what people thought and overall, I stopped considering my own feelings. I had to activate self-love. It helped me to accept everything about me, flaws and all.

Once you start to accept yourself, you become aware of your very own strengths and weaknesses. You start to take inventory of your health, talents and your capabilities despite the deficiencies or flaws, you think you see.

For you created my inmost being; you knit me together in my mother's womb. I praise you because I am fearfully and wonderfully made -Psalm 139:13-14.

Self-acceptance is satisfaction or contentment with yourself and your overall life in general. It is a fundamental pillar of mental health and well-being. It involves a realistic understanding and appreciation of one's strengths and weaknesses. Someone who has developed self-acceptance recognizes their unique worth and has a compassionate attitude towards themselves. They know their limits, but they are not held back by limiting beliefs.

Many people struggle with self-acceptance, and are not able to love, accept, or forgive themselves. I want to write about this because self-acceptance is needed to be happy with who you are in life. I think about how I don't want to look back on my life years from now and reflect on all of the opportunities I may have missed because I was too self-conscious about something small, or too shy to be myself.

To me, self-acceptance means to forgive yourself for not being perfect. To be good to yourself and do things that inspire you to love yourself. Despite all the things you think may be wrong with you. Because you have self-love, you can show yourself compassion.

Everything becomes more difficult in life if you are not willing to accept yourself for who you are. You're unhappy, you lack trust in yourself, and you develop a victim mentality. Furthermore, If you do not accept yourself, you may believe what others tell you, instead of believing your own voice.

Each day is a new opportunity to strive to be the very best version of you. Why should we waste time putting ourselves down? When the truth is there is always going to be someone smarter, prettier, someone more athletic and someone "better". We all have our faults, but that doesn't give us a reason to think of ourselves as unworthy or undeserving of happiness. We are who we are, and individuality is an important value to recognize.

NO ONE HAS WRONGED ME...MORE THAN ME

Let's Look Within!

What would you like to change about yourself and why?

_____

_____

_____

_____

_____

_____

_____

_____

What are some flaws that you dislike about yourself?

_____

_____

_____

_____

_____

_____

_____

_____

_____

_____

_____

_____

_____

_____

What do you need to accept about yourself that you
have rejected?

_____

_____

_____

_____

_____

_____

_____

_____

What compliment do you receive the most?

_____

_____

_____

_____

_____

_____

_____

_____

What is your least favorite attribute about yourself?

_____

_____

_____

_____

_____

_____

_____

_____

_____

_____

_____

_____

_____

_____

A Prayer of Self-Acceptance

Dear Divine,

Help me accept myself as I am.

Amen

Affirmation

*I choose to let go of pain and focus on **healing** all aspect of my inner **child**.*

*I am thankful for all the ways my inner **child** has helped me become more **in** alignment with my true self.*

I love my inner child unconditionally.

Healing My Inner Child

"I'm not the average girl from your video, and I ain't built like a supermodel, but I learned to love myself unconditionally, because I am a Queen" **-India Arie**

This chapter is about healing the little girl within you. God has a purpose for each and every one of us. To walk effectively in our purpose, we have to work on healing those things that binds us. The starting point to healing begins with self. Before we can be honest with anyone else, we must be honest with ourselves. Honesty with yourself, begins with making the mirror your best friend. I started looking within to ask God the most important questions and then I asked myself some questions.

Ask God for Wisdom (Even at a young age).

If any of you lacks wisdom, you should ask God, who gives generously to all without finding fault, and it will be given to you. James 1:5

I love my mirror talks. The conversations take courage and transparency. As a little girl my imagination fostered an image of myself that was completely opposite of what I looked like. As a little girl, my perception of how I looked stemmed from what I thought was the ideal skin tone- being "light skinned".

In the 80s, the popular term "melanin poppin" wasn't trending, and having a darker skin tone wasn't celebrated like it is today. I had an internalized image of myself, that didn't represent who I was. How I envisioned myself was not at all who I was. I hated the color of my skin tone. So, I would imagine myself as a light skinned girl with long hair.

My perception of self was a generational view of what my family thought, as well as society's views attractiveness. I didn't understand the impact that society's standard of beauty had on how I saw myself, however these were the painful memories of my past. I was a brown skin girl, who wanted to be light skin with long hair. That's the image I saw mostly on TV, and those were the women who appeared on Billboards.

Being light skinned seem to be highly celebrated or talked about. At family gatherings someone would make a comment about being light-skinned. This is why it is important for parents and caregivers to be aware of their own internalized views about skin tone and hair texture because their views can inadvertently affect their children's development of a positive racial identity and self-concept.

So, in my youthful imagination when I thought about what beauty looks like, I developed an image in my head. It wasn't until I went to college that I began to celebrate my individuality and beauty. I began to see that true beauty is when you accept the very essence of who you were made to be.

I stood in front of the mirror every day before I showered and began breaking down the negative thought patterns and poor habits that I created about myself. I would do this through positive affirmations. I started treating myself the way I deserved to be treated. I was loving on myself the way I deserved to be loved. I began to be at peace with who I was; every fiber of my being, every aspect of my life, understanding that I am perfect just the way God made me. Even through my imperfections! I had to accept my individual beauty; my skin tone, every physical feature, even my acne, *every pimple on my face, is where it's supposed to be.*

Self-acceptance allowed me to heal the child within. I had to show myself compassion and had to realize that the person who needed forgiving the most was myself. When you are at peace with who you are, it removes the mask and the burden of self-comparison.

I encourage young girls to be at peace with the person God made them to be! Self-love allowed me to see past my flaws and imperfections. You have power! If there's anything within your control to change, you have to power to change it. I said the serenity prayer each morning to create a positive mind set. The Serenity

Prayer was a powerful prayer that I learned growing up, *God grant me the serenity to accept the things I cannot change Courage to accept the things I can and the Wisdom to know the difference.*

Healing the little girl within is about coming to peace with the past trauma from your childhood. Healing those things from my past meant forgiving myself for the very thoughts that I created, that formed damaging belief systems not in alignment with who God created me to be. I had to unlearn the negative words I spoke and replaced them with high powerful words.

I had to forgive myself for the things that were beyond my control, and I took full responsibility. To start the journey of healing the little girl inside started with having a real conversation with myself and forgiving myself and accepting false belief systems that were simply not true. This false belief system had me thinking that I wasn't pretty and believing that no one else would think I was beautiful. Because of those belief systems, it challenged my self-confidence as a little girl. I had to forgive myself for not realizing my beauty, my talent, and forgetting that God has made me wonderful.

To undo some of those damaging beliefs, I spoke life into myself. I started with positive affirmations and speaking healing words. I started to realize that there were some past traumas that I needed to come face to face with and started telling myself what I needed to hear all along. I wish I had adults around back then that saw the hurt on the inside as a little girl. Adults who would have spoken life into me. I started to realize that there were some past traumas that I needed to come face to face with and started telling myself what I needed to hear all along.

Each day was a new opportunity to speak positive affirmations and to tell myself that I was beautiful. And to not just say it, but to sit with it, believe it and if there was any doubtful encounter, I would quickly bring down those negative thoughts with God's truth about me.

Life and Death are in the power of your tongue -Proverbs 18:21

Again, words are powerful. The bible instructs us that Life and death are in the power of your tongue. There is power in the words we speak. We have the power to either speak beautiful things about ourselves or to speak ugly words towards ourselves.

As a mother, I vow to fill in those gaps for my little girls by striving to keep my cup full so that I can pour into their lives and speak life into their hearts. It's up to us as the caregivers, as parents, as role models to speak life into our children.

The words we speak to ourselves contribute to the way we see ourselves. I believe the more we speak positive words, the more they will resonate with us and we will then believe them. Pay attention to the very words that you release. Are they used to build up or are your words used to tear down?

When I started the healing journey, addressing past trauma and healing the little girl within, I wrote a letter to myself every day. In the letters, I asked for forgiveness for whatever negative thoughts I had of myself. I wrote words of affirmation and affirmed things that truly represented me. This healing process allowed me to accept the woman I am today.

Let's Look Within!

What are some encouraging words you can tell your younger self?

_____

_____

_____

_____

_____

_____

_____

_____

What advice would you give to a young person you may know?

_____

_____

_____

_____

_____

_____

_____

_____

_____

_____

_____

_____

_____

Fast forwards 10-20 years from now, what advice could you give your future self?

_____

_____

_____

_____

_____

_____

_____

How has your inner child helped you to align with your true self?

_____

_____

_____

_____

_____

_____

_____

_____

_____

_____

_____

_____

_____

_____

_____

What are some ways your childhood has help to
shape you into the person you are today?

_____

_____

_____

_____

_____

_____

_____

NO ONE HAS WRONGED ME...MORE THAN ME

Prayer

Dear Divine,

I love you with all of my heart, mind, and soul!

Help me to heal the past traumas of my life so that I can fully express your love!

Amen!

Affirmation

I am a beautiful soul

I honor my mother and my father

I accept who I am

Healing the Mother Wound

This chapter is dedicated to opening the heart to healing the mother wound. It's about forgiveness and making the connection to healing the little girl within. It's no secret, the mother-daughter relationship can be a challenging one. Cultivating this relationship is a healthy part of a young girl's growth.

My mother is one of the strongest women I know. Growing up, life wasn't perfect. I grew up seeing my mother struggle. Life wasn't easy, but the love and protection of our mama was matchless. However, there were times, I felt a deep disconnection from my mother. As a teenager, I felt that my mother didn't understand me. I was constantly seeking approval. I was the middle child and my mother's oldest daughter. This disconnection made me feel that I wasn't good enough. I wanted to be seen and heard by my mother. At that age, I didn't know how to articulate my feelings, so I took it out on mama in ways that a young teenage girl would.

As a teenager, I was unhappy and angry, and I blamed my mom for almost everything that went wrong in my life. I was your typical teen, sassy with a smart mouth. I internalized the issues that my mom and dad had and made them my own.

We grew up in the projects. Mama raised six of us as a single mother. Daddy was around, but it was mama who was the caretaker. Many days I saw mama manage to deal with her own struggles. From just being a woman and mother, struggling to provide the best life for her children, the best as she knew how. My mother made many sacrifices and I couldn't fathom enduring the things she had to overcome. She did it so her kids wouldn't have to. She had to fight to overcome her own struggles in life and push through past traumas.

My mother made sure to provide for her children's physical needs, she made sure we had a roof over our heads and food on the table. We had some good days and we had some bad days. But we lacked the emotional support needed from mama. Mama was emotionally unavailable because she was still fighting through her own issues. I wanted to have the bond with my mama that I would hear from my friends at school. They raved about their mother being their best friend, and I wanted that. These feelings carried throughout my teenaged years made life a bit challenging to say the least.

Times where I needed my mother emotionally, she was unavailable, perhaps swept away by the stresses of life. That is what the mother wound is, it is the emotional absence of your mother during your growing years. Life has a way of keeping us from being present and in the moment if we allow it to. When you are dealing with struggles, it derails you from focusing on things that are important. I was the middle child, having two older brothers and three younger sisters, waiting to be seen and to be heard. At times I felt invisible.

Simply put mama had her own mess to deal, at least that's how I internalize things. Growing up I realize that this disconnection created some deep mother wounds that needed healing. I especially recognized this as I began my journey into womanhood and became a mother of my own children.

What is the mother wound? The mother wound is the set of painful patterns originating with our mothers that caused us to unconsciously limit or sabotage ourselves.

Challenges between mothers and daughters are not always talked about. It's still a sore subject, and most conflicts are resolved with time. As little girls, our mothers are our first teachers. We learned from our mothers, we gleaned from our mothers, we are taught about womanhood from our mothers. As young girls, we are watching, and we are learning. We learn how to process our traumas from watching the women before us. As women, we either repeat these behaviors by doing exactly what they did, or we commit to changing the narrative of our story.

Growing up, I watched my mother and paid close attention to her. To be honest, I didn't always get a good glimpse of what love is or should be. I watched the women before me give more than they received, neglecting their own worthiness to be loved by a man. I watched them forsake their purpose on a mission to satisfy others. I watched them neglect their own destiny for pleasure. I witnessed unrequited love. I witnessed the lack of reciprocity, I witnessed them putting themselves on the back burner and putting him first.

As a result, I was a mess. Because of this I vowed to never lose myself to the hands of a man. I vowed to be different. But instead, what I saw formed some bad agreements within. It taught me how not to love myself. The only way I could break this cycle was to love me the way I wanted to be loved. That is the key. What a journey this has been. Self-love is liberating. I hold space for women who neglect their worthiness, I mourn for broken women trying to care for a broken man, it can't be done. As a little girl I was a student, and in retrospect, what I learned was self-love. These were the mother wounds that needed healing.

I began to heal the mother wound, when I became a mother. It's something about womanhood and motherhood that makes you understand that not only was she my mother, but she was also a woman, she was human. I internalized my mother's struggle and I made them my own, and for a long time I resented her for our struggles and blamed her for a lot of the negative aspects from my childhood. This belief that I developed affected our relationship a great deal, it also affected my relationship with myself.

When I started to grow, I realized that I needed to heal the mother wound so that I could stop the cycle with my own children. I had to first forgive myself for carrying those wounds and feelings of unworthiness and feelings of being unloved as a child. As I got older, I was able to resonate with my mother in so many ways, and those wounds started to heal because I was able to see past my mother's pain. Forgiving was liberating. I was able to understand her as a woman. I saw her as a woman for the first time. That understanding led me to healing the pain created from my relationship with my mother. Like all mother-daughter relationships, I recognize that it wasn't easy raising a teen daughter. That relationship can be a difficult relationship to navigate. It created some tension and resentment between the two of us.

When I had my daughter, I knew I needed to heal this wound. The wounds that my mother carried over the years passed along to me. These wounds consisted of toxic belief systems that were formed.

Unhealed mother wounds can result in a cycle of abusive behavior with self. It can create comparison with other females, self-sabotaging, not having any boundaries or always saying yes when you should say no. This toxic trait leads to you putting others before yourself, being codependent in relationships, failed relationships, inability to form healthy relationship with other females and silences you so that you are afraid to use your authentic voice.

It is important that we understand how much our mothers have gone through in the face of these oppressive ideas and expectations. It is important that we realize that no mother can be perfect no matter how hard they try and use this knowledge to generate forgiveness.

Today, the relationship with my mother is stronger than ever before. My mother is my best friend and I am even more amazed at her strength and how she handled life. Because of her, I am the woman I am today.

Let's Look Within!

Take a moment and think about the kind of relationship you have with your mother, what is it like?

_____

_____

_____

_____

_____

_____

_____

What would make your relationship with your mother better?

_____

_____

_____

_____

_____

_____

_____

What are some healthy boundaries that you set for yourself?

_____

_____

_____

_____

_____

_____

_____

_____

What are some false beliefs that you may have developed as a result of the relationship you have with your mother?

_____

_____

_____

_____

_____

_____

_____

Healing the Mother Wound Prayer

Dear Divine,

I love you with all of my heart, mind, soul, and strength.

Thank you for allowing the relationship that I have with my mother to align with your divine order.

It is in you that I live, breath, and have my being.

Amen

Affirmation

I AM Perfectly Imperfect

I am all who God says I am

I walk with confidence

I speak with confidence

I am a confident

CONFIDENCE IN ME

"Confidence is knowing your value, instead of proving your worth"-Unknown

I wasn't always confident.

When you don't understand your value and your worth, you definitely struggle with self-confidence! My struggle with self-confidence was the result of self-doubt! Doubting who I was, my talents and abilities, who I was becoming, and what I was capable of achieving. My own feelings of inadequacy and self-doubt contributed to my lack of confidence in many areas of my life. The thing about confidence was, there were areas where I was very confident, and others where I lacked confidence.

I developed a passion for singing and writing songs at such a young age. You start off with a winning attitude, and because we sometimes reach for perfection, we gradually lose confidence when things don't turn out the way we expected. The easiest option sometimes is to give up. It took me a while to build confidence in sharing my talent. The more you practice and show love to your gift, the more confident you become. Building confidence for me was about self-belief and self-love.

Things have to perfect in order for dreams to come true.

This negative belief system kept me from going after the things that I was passionate about. Everything you've ever wanted is right outside of your comfort zone. Too often we get caught up in thinking that certain things have to happen in order to make dreams come true, when all we need is confidence and determination. It's in our hands.

Building self-confidence is being aware of your struggles and making a commitment to yourself to do something about it. Often times when we look in the mirror, we are deceived to think that we need to be perfect in order for things to happen. We have conditioned ourselves to believe that certain things have to be in order to reach goals, or two complete something. What we must realize is that motivation is spurred with action.

It's not about the absence of problems or the absence of struggles, it is the mindset that you have that will allow you to work towards something in the midst of those struggles. That's what confidence is to me. Self-confidence is about believing in yourself, believing in your qualities, talents and trusting your judgment to make things happen and being sure of that.

Self-confidence is the courage to know yourself, believe in yourself, and act on your beliefs. Self-confidence is a positive feeling about yourself and the world that leads to courageous actions born out of a sense of self-respect. Self-confidence is having the courage to know yourself, believe in yourself and to act on your beliefs.

Once you set a goal or make yourself a promise to achieve your goals, your confidence is really the vehicle to reaching that goal. It's how you see yourself; it's about knowing and accepting yourself.

As a teenager, this was an area I really had to work through. This was because of the feelings of unworthiness that I carried. A lack of self-confidence can stem from a past trauma in your childhood and your background. I did not always believe in myself. I would start something but never saw it to the finish line. And that's one thing about confidence, it's about seeing and believing in yourself, visualizing how you are going to reach those goals you have set for yourself. Self-confidence is setting your mark and racing towards the finish line. If you set out to do something, make sure you see it to completion. Be sure that no matter what you are committed to, see it through to completion or else you will end up cheating yourself. Even if it doesn't happen the way you want it to happen or it doesn't pan out the way you have in mind, the achievement of a goal or accomplishing something, gives you more and more confidence to keep building and to keep going.

For example, let's say you set a goal to become an avid runner, however, you've never ran before and really don't think you can do it. You are not as confident that you can pull this off because you've never actually ran. The things that we've never done can definitely have an impact on our confidence. However, you build confidence by setting small task to reach the bigger goal. This task may look like running in intervals and then resting or including a walk/run regime until you can run your course non-stop. The more you work at it, the more you develop confidence. Building self-confidence means pushing yourself out of your comfort zone and toward your goals. You will start to feel better about the goal of becoming a runner because you were able to achieve small victories along the way.

If at first you don't succeed, dust yourself off and try again. When you lack confidence, you are more likely to develop these limiting thought processes or belief systems that you can't do a certain thing because, well, you may not be accustomed to it, or you may have tried and failed. When it comes to failure, there's really never failure, there are opportunities to improve and lessons to be learned. Each time you try to do something new, even if there is a mistake, you learn what you did wrong, you go back, and you do it again.

It's important as parents, mentors, teachers or anyone who has a charge over young people to speak to our younger people. Speak Life into them letting them know that you believe in them when they don't have the capacity to believe in themselves. It takes those around us, our support system to pour into our young people.

Let's Look Within!

Think about some positive words you would like to
speak over your life! Let's start with the I AM factor.
Fill in with words of affirmations

I AM

_____

_____

I AM

_____

_____

I AM

_____

_____

I AM

_____

_____

I AM

_____

_____

Prayer

Dear Divine,

I give you all of my insecurities, my self-doubts and fears. Please help me to trust and believe in myself as I know you are working through me and I do trust and believe in you.

Amen

Affirmations

The I AM Factor

I am beautiful

I am loved

I am supported

I am abundant

I am fierce

I am brave

I am confident

I am creative

I am talented

I am joy

Words are Powerful

If words of affirmation were like food on the table and clothes on my back, then I went plenty of days hungry and half-naked. I'm not saying that we didn't show love in our family, it was understood. Surely, we loved each other. The caveat was we didn't always know how to express our love verbally.

The power of your voice

Affirmations are so important in a young person's growth. As important it is for parents to speak affirming words to their children, it's just as important and empowering for young people **to be taught** how to create positive beliefs in themselves so that they are not easily torn down when others try to hurt them.

It's important to be taught how to love and affirm ourselves even as young children. Not hearing words that affirm my true essence had an impact on my esteem. Not being told that I was beautiful enough affected my self-esteem.

Before I even began a task, the resistance in me, would come up with a thousand reasons why it could not be done, especially if it was something that I had not done previously. I developed this belief system even before I even tried things. I created limiting beliefs and talked myself out of doing something before I gave it a try. I am so glad that God is not bound to my limited thinking and belief system.

Just because you haven't done it before, doesn't mean it can't be done

You have a voice! You have to be careful not to believe what other people say about you, that's why it's important for you to know who you are inside and out. When people say something positive about you it should resonate with you if it's true, so that you can confirm what you already know. Likewise, when there is something about you that you know need changing, you can accept the constructive criticism, and take the steps to make those changes.

As you grow and heal, never allow someone to tell you something about yourself that you didn't already know. Sometimes the people around us who love us remind us of things that we already know about our self, and other times, they can plant seeds of doubt that just aren't true. When you know who you are, you are less likely to subscribe to a false narrative that someone may have attempted to create about you.

Self-confidence is a state of being certain of who you are and believing that the course of action you chose is the best or most effective.

Self-confidence is about being certain of what you want and how you want to go about getting what you want. There are no questions asked and no room for doubt. Self-confidence eliminates self-doubt.

Being a teenager can be hard. It can be a difficult space to navigate as you are developing your self-identity. During my teenage years my confidence was challenged. My sister and I started a singing group and we would perform in the city. We practiced daily and were really excited about making it "big".

We were so focused on our goal of making our dreams come true, yet it was during this time, where my confidence in singing really started taking a back seat. I became an introvert, especially when it came to singing. Comparison reared its ugly head, and I would often compare myself to my sister's voice. She was the soprano and I was the alto. I had yet to find my own voice and appreciate my lower registry. I was struggling with lack of self-love, and low self-esteem was deeply rooted within me.

The music industry is a harsh world, and if not protected and taught how to navigate through, it can become vicious and weigh heavily on your self-worth.

During a singing event at a talent showcase, my sister and I were set to go on stage and perform a song we wrote and arranged. I vividly remember being heckled from someone in the crowd who pointed out so poignantly, that I couldn't sing in comparison to my sister. It was at that moment where I allowed a stranger's voice to completely shatter my confidence.

Feeling embarrassed, I needed that instant support of loved one's around who could speak life into me. Imagine, lacking the values and principles of self-love and self-worth when you are met with a stranger's voice, who tells you something different about yourself than who you really are. Simply put, you don't have the tools needed to repel those negative words and no one to affirm you in the moment. I allowed someone else, a complete stranger, to shake my belief system about who I was, and it affected my confidence for a long time. I gave up. I thought I wasn't good enough. And I was on to the next. I found a replacement and put all of my energy into doing something else.

Slowly, I lost my zeal for singing and performing. I thought that if I just focused on something else, I was good at, I would be ok. It was also during that time, that I lost my passion for writing. Instead of stretching myself to work towards my dream, I took a seat in my comfort zone and rested there for a while. Sitting in your comfort zone doesn't help you build confidence you just become comfortable and complacent with what you already know.

I admire those who are not the most skilled at certain things. Those who are not the best at something, yet they are confident to go out and do whatever it is that they set their mind to. Perfection and confidence are not related. You don't have to be perfect at something to be confident, in fact, it's the complete opposite. My lack of self-confidence was steeped in feelings of unworthiness. Paralyzed by those limiting beliefs that everything had to be perfect in order to be valued.

Self-confidence inspires other people to be confident as well. When you are a confident girl, you shine bright. You stand out in the crowd. You glow differently. When others see you and how you value yourself, the energy is transferable.

*But blessed is the one who trusts in **the Lord**, whose **confidence** is in him -Jeremiah 17:7*

Let's Look Within!

Who are the people in your life who encourages you?

_____

_____

_____

_____

_____

_____

_____

_____

What makes you feel good about yourself?

_____

_____

_____

_____

_____

_____

_____

_____

_____

What are some things that you personally feel like you are not good at?

_____

_____

_____

_____

_____

_____

_____

_____

What are somethings you would like to improve about yourself?

_____

_____

_____

_____

_____

_____

_____

_____

_____

_____

What are your strengths or good qualities?

_____

_____

_____

_____

_____

_____

_____

What are some bad habits that you know of that you can break?

_____

_____

_____

_____

_____

_____

_____

_____

_____

What positive habits can you develop to build your
self-confidence and self-esteem?

_____

_____

_____

_____

_____

_____

_____

_____

_____

_____

_____

_____

_____

_____

_____

_____

_____

_____

PAMELA RENEE GUNN

Dear Divine,
Your grace is sufficient for me, your power is made perfect in weakness. Help me to see myself as YOU see me. I am wonderfully made. Help me to think of myself as YOU think of me. Therefore, I will boast all the more gladly about my weaknesses, so that your power may rest on me. For when I am weak, then I am strong.
Amen

Affirmation

I forgive myself completely

I let go and will allow my heart to heal

I forgive those who have hurt me

I forgive myself for hurting me

Self-Forgiveness

I owe myself an apology for all of the self-hate I inflicted on myself as a little girl! I owe myself an apology for not seeing my own beauty, and for thinking I wasn't enough! I owe myself an apology for feelings of unworthiness. I am now committed to healing and being the woman, I needed when I was younger!

The cure to self-hate is simple, self-love. I realized the amount of damage I had done to myself throughout my childhood years. I knew I had to ask God for forgiveness first, and then I had to go through a process where I forgave myself. Self-forgiveness wasn't easy because it was a self-realization that no one had done me wrong, more than I had done me wrong. After all of these years asking God why, he revealed that *healing starts with me.*

I was the solution to the problems I inflicted on myself. I began to be real with myself and it freed me from falling victim to things outside of my control and blaming others. I had to rewrite the blueprint. Once again, my mirror talk was about realizing all the times I was hard on myself, the times where I would self-sabotage and deny the very essence of who I was. I had to acknowledge the times where I had given space to the enemy, for the suicidal thoughts, for the reckoning and damaging relationship with my own self, for denying my beauty, dishonoring my ancestors- I had to forgive. I had to forgive myself for not treating myself like I mattered and for honoring a stranger's voice before my own. I had to forgive me. This was not easy, and there were plenty of days where I felt a force of resistance, but I had to persevere. I owed myself an apology for not honoring my own voice, for saying yes, when deep down I should have said no.

Forgiveness is powerful. First God, then self, then others. Forgiveness liberated me to forgive everyone who I thought were against me. But before I could forgive anyone else, I had to make amends with me. I started to heal and gain back my strength. I began to use my voice. I fell in love again, in love with me.

Self- forgiveness means that you have accepted the behaviors that were not conducive to your growth and that you are willing to move past it, to move forward. It means you have accepted what has happened in the past and you're making an agreement with yourself that you are willing to learn the lessons to grow.

Self-sabotage is the worst form of self-hate and emotional abuse. Self-sabotage had me blaming myself. What happens when you blame yourself;

according to Michael Formica, is that self-blame amplifies our perceived inadequacies, whether real or imagined, and paralyzes us before we can even begin to move forward.

Through this process I had to shake free from the weight or the gravity of not knowing who I was. I had to break loose from the gravity of not knowing myself to the fullest. I had to shake free even from the regret of all of those years of self-doubt and self-hate and self-sabotage and I had to be free in order to grow into the woman that God intended for me to be.

Liberation is powerful. There is something so magical about when you know that you have been forgiven. Like a child who knows that they've done something wrong and when they are confronted by their parents, instead of being reprimanded, they are forgiven.

Self-forgiveness is about living in the now, living in the moment without being weighed down from your past. It's a deliberate decision to let go. Letting go of the resentment, the anger and the retribution that you made against yourself and those who have wronged you.

We have to be mindful when we can be so forgiving towards others yet it's hard for us to forgive ourselves. Self-sabotage paralyzed me. Forgiving myself gave me mobility. It was what I needed to get my breakthrough. Self-forgiveness started with me taking action. Faith without action is useless. I had to put some action to my faith.

Self-forgiveness started with accepting personal responsibility. I had to release the propensity to blame others. I released the blame that I placed on my parents for my upbringing. I could no longer blame my childhood because self-love freed me from riding the blame wave. I no longer blamed my childhood, I had to accept personal responsibility for the things in my life that I knew needed changing.

Life gives us so many lessons, one of those great lessons is learning how to master the art of personal responsibility. It is so powerful, yet many people (adults) fail to accept personal responsibility for the consequences of life, based on the decisions they've made. It's all about the lesson. When we stop pointing the finger and being angry at the very ones that love and support us throughout this journey, we will begin to heal, learn, and benefit from those lessons if we simply look at the person in the mirror and accept personal responsibility. You have to make the mirror your best friend. Life is a full circle, full of second chances. Ask for wisdom and understanding, humble yourself, and get back on track.

The next step in self-forgiveness was realizing that a change needed to happen a change needed to take place. I had to visualize what this change looked like for me. Self-forgiveness included me actually verbalizing and speaking aloud and hearing myself say, "I'm sorry for…"

I had to realize that it was not about failure it was about learning. When you ask the question, God will give you answers. It may not be what we expect, but we always receive the answer. We just have to listen. I started to ask questions like, what lesson am I supposed to learn from all of this. This was necessary to move forward.

I've diminished my authentic voice more times than I can remember. I've given my "Yes" to people and things that should have received my "No". As a result, I've dealt with regret and resentment because of it. I am missioned minded and no longer will I allow the matters of the heart to override what God has for me. When you dishonor your authentic voice, you invite distractions into your life. You wrestle with the heart. Your heart wants to say yes, but you are called to focus on the mission at hand. God reminds me daily that this battle is not mine and that we must trust God and his plans for our lives.

Let's Look Within!

What do you need to forgive yourself for?

_____
_____
_____
_____
_____
_____
_____
_____

What ways have you wronged yourself?

_____
_____
_____
_____
_____
_____
_____
_____

What are some healthy boundaries that you set for yourself?

_____

_____

_____

_____

_____

_____

_____

_____

_____

What are some steps you will take to forgive yourself?

_____

_____

_____

_____

_____

_____

_____

_____

_____

Prayer

Dear Divine,

I love you with all of my Heart, Mind, and Soul and Strength.

I receive your love

Because I have YOUR love, I am able to love deeply and completely

Your love allows me to forgive myself today.

I release all of the hurt and pain I have caused myself.

I surrender to your love and will for my life.

Amen.

Affirmation

From this moment on, I am free

I am free from the pain and abuse of self-hate and self-sabotage

I am enough

I am beautiful

I am confident

I forgive myself

I am whole, healthy, and complete, lacking nothing!

Falling in Love with the Woman I've Become

Music heals. The healing power of music has always served me well. Music has helped me to better love myself, and because of that, music has and is still a part of my healing journey.

Today I am in love with the woman God has made me to be. I am still learning, I am still healing, and growing. I recognize that there is still work to do. I am a student, and life is my teacher. My love for music is still strong. I often go to my sacred space and just let the music breath. Whenever there is something surfacing that is not in alignment with who I am, I have the tools to bring me back to my center.

I am thankful for the musical influences of Lalah Hathaway who shared with me that you have to make the mirror your best friend. She sang to me (through her song) and said, *"Bitter hearts don't hold a smile Troubled Minds will wear you down, Use your past to get ahead, Hold your tears and think instead, Have to find a way to make it, These clouds, Are letting up for a while, Sometimes you got to make, The mirror your best friend, And maybe then, You'll find some peace within, Stop hiding yourself, Love yourself, When no one else can".*

I grew up on the staple singers who all spoke to me through their music. The Great Mrs. Aretha Franklin who told me to *"Respect Myself".* India Arie reminded me to love my "*Brown Skin*" and reminded me of what I already had, *"Strength, Courage, and Wisdom".* And Mary J. Blige told me that I had to love myself before I could love anyone else, and Whitney Houston told me that *The Greatest Love of All* was easy to achieve. Music has always been a part of me. It was through music, I was able to dream and go to places through the melodies and harmonies and lyrics.

I now accept that which I thought was my weakness is actually my strength. My vulnerability is strength, my transparency is strength, my intuition is a gift! Today, I am highly esteemed. I speak life into my being. The moment I realized that comparing myself and competing with others undermined my self-value and self-worth, healing began.

My current vibe is SELF-CARE, raising my children, satisfying my husband, drinking lots of water, taking care of my skin, balancing life and work, drinking my tea, journaling, writing my books, enrolling into a good PhD program, writing songs, taking care of this temple, eating healthy, managing my blood sugar, taking care of my mental, taking bubble baths, soaking my feet, exercising, repelling negative energy, being present, showing up, enjoying life, getting better every day and doing all things that are the makings of me. I am no longer repressed by low self-esteem. I have the gift of expression. I compete with no one but me, working on bettering myself daily is work, but I'm committed. I don't have the space to focus on what others are doing, I AM ENOUGH.

Self-love is the next best thing to God's love. It's a daily walk. While we are constantly taught to show love to others, we often fail in extending it to ourselves; that frequency comes in the form of self-neglect. In order to love each other effectively, we must first learn to love ourselves. Today, I practice self-love. It has become the caveat to overcoming all inner struggles.

Today, I embrace the woman I've become. Accepting every fiber of my being is who I am, is who God created me to be. When I honor myself, I am honoring the women before me. I am in the habit of repelling any and everything that tries to hinder and stop my growth.

It's not about the absence of problems, it's having the tools to overcome. Even on this healing journey, remnants of old though patterns and insecurities will come. The things that use to trip me up, I now walk over. What seemed to hold me down for what seemed like an eternity, I now bounce back better and stronger. That is what healing looks like! Healing is drawing strength from within, knowing you have

Power. For God did not give you the spirit of fear, but of love, power and a sound mind.

In so many ways, I see myself in my children. They have helped me heal the little girl within me. I make promises to them.   My promises to my daughters are that I will always remind them of their beauty and their strength. It is my goal to always offer words of affirmation, to encourage and to build them up. I want my son and my daughter to be confident knowing that they have an extraordinary gift on the inside. When we teach our girls to love who they are and to be confident in all they do, we are then creating a world full of strong and whole women, who love themselves and are able to raise a generation of women who will do the same.

Made in the USA
Columbia, SC
24 November 2020

25417645R00067